PRECIOUS MOMENTS

PRECIOUS MOMENTS

Elaine Murray

ATHENA PRESS
LONDON

Precious Moments
Copyright © Elaine Murray 2009

All Rights Reserved

No part of this book may be reproduced in any form
by photocopying or by any electronic or mechanical means,
including information storage or retrieval systems,
without permission in writing from both the copyright
owner and the publisher of this book.

ISBN 978 1 84748 601 1

First published 2009 by
ATHENA PRESS
Queen's House, 2 Holly Road
Twickenham TW1 4EG
United Kingdom

Printed for Athena Press

To my daughter, Hollie, for her support and for helping me with my numerous grammatical errors, which she found highly amusing – I love you so much.

I would like to thank my husband, Paul, for the love and support he always gives me, for cooking dinner and doing so much more, so that I had time to put all my memories together – I love you so much.

To my son Dylan for his encouragement and love towards me and my work – I love you so much.

To my son Quinten for his inspiration and his openness in sharing his wisdom with me – I love you so much.

To my dear friend Marie McAlavey for her support, encouragement, patience and many cups of coffee – thank you, I love you.

To Athena Press for being open to receiving me and my angels and for having the belief and confidence in us to take our work to publication.

To my angels, loved ones and friends in the spirit world for coming to me each day – thank you, I love you.

And especially to God for allowing me to have this communication – I love you so much.

The stories that I have told in this book are life lessons. The stories that I experienced were life-changing.

I would like to introduce you to a few of my angelic moments.

I hope that you enjoy reading them as much as I enjoy having them to share with you.

I have been writing in diaries ever since I can remember. I always found writing was a form of therapy for me. I felt any situation was lighter after I had poured my heart out on paper. It was like having a best friend – someone waiting to listen to me. It always helped me to relax and be myself. Once I started to write, I could not stop until all that was in my heart was shared with my diary. The pages were covered with tears of joy, but when I felt vulnerable was when I got my greatest comfort from writing. I could write for hours and would often fall asleep because there was such a release for me. When I had my children, the amount of time I had for writing in my diary became less and less and I often longed to sit with my old friend and share my life.

Then, in 1997, I hit a personal crisis in my life. My husband lost his job and our lives were thrown into turmoil. Some days were a blur; I could not see any light at the end of the tunnel for us. And with two young children it all seemed so much harder. End it all seemed the only possible release from the torment. It was only the strong love that I had for my family that kept me going. I had to hold on and try to find a way to get things together again. Love is a very powerful tool and it pulled me through my darkest days.

One night, I cried out to my grandmother who had passed over a few years earlier. We were very close and

I loved her so much. 'I need you, Nan!' I cried. 'I miss you so much; help me, please.'

As I climbed the stairs to go to bed, I felt her behind me. As I sat on the bed, my body drained of energy. 'Oh Nan,' I sobbed, 'I need you so much now.' That's when I saw a male figure at my right-hand side. I wiped my tears to try and clear my eyes; I thought I was seeing things. I asked, 'Who are you?'

'I am Archangel Michael.'

All I could see was his head and shoulders. His smile was so brilliant. I just felt so peaceful. 'I brought your grandmother.' I looked to my left – it was Nan. She wrapped her arms around me just the very way she used to hold me. I cried and cried into her shoulder but she told me everything would be OK, that she and Archangel Michael would help us. I looked around to see if he was still there and he was.

'You are never alone, Elaine,' he said. 'We see and hear you and you will go on. Life can be challenging and hard, but you have much to do here. Time will show you many reasons for our visit to you.'

His words were like a comfort blanket; his smile spoke volumes. I turned to Nan and she said, 'I have something I want to share with you and you can keep it for ever.'

I'll Be There

> I see your life from my home in heaven, I
>   watch you from afar.
> I see you grieve and cry for me and I wonder
>   how you are.

> I turned to God and asked him to please allow me to go,
> To be by your side and help comfort you just for a while so you'd know.
> You'd feel me near and hear my voice in little whispers in your ear
> And when you'd close your eyes at night I would be there.
> God promised to allow me this time for us to share.
> Have faith, I am with you – I'm never really gone.
> I'll walk with you for ever and, when your time is done,
> You'll walk with me and the angels and return to God's call
> And you will realise: I was never really gone at all.

'Nan, that was so beautiful; the love that was going through me then was so good.'

I saw them starting to fade and I knew they were leaving. I thanked them; that night changed my life for ever.

Life was good again we had another baby and I knew that Nan was still around me. I would feel her come into a room and I would talk to her. I was opening up into a whole new world, talking to spirit.

To get my attention, my lights would go on and off, the radio had a mind of its own and the spirit of my beloved dog Tia, who had passed over, would come and run in around my legs in a figure-of-eight motion. I would say, 'Hi, Tia, I love and miss you.'

Being a mum to three young children kept me really busy, but I know now that the spirit world and the angels were always close. But it always felt like they were stepping back to allow me to be a mum; their approach was gentle and yet constant.

I always felt that there was more to my life, that there was something I should be doing, but I trusted that I would be told when the time was right.

One night, after I settled the children in bed, my husband, Paul, was at work. I flopped into my chair. I was tired and enjoying the moment of stillness. Suddenly, I heard an angel asking me to start writing again. I couldn't see the angel, but I felt him kneel beside my chair. He wanted me to write about my conversation with the angels and the spirit world. He called it my 'angelic awakening'. I trusted the voice – I didn't know why, at the time, I just knew the angels had a plan for my writing.

It had been a long time since I had written anything

down. I went and got my pen and paper and sat down. The angel was still there and this is what he asked me to write:

The Awakening

> Have you wondered about the whispers,
> The soft brush of our wings,
> The nudges and the feelings
> And all the other little things –
> The white feathers you asked for,
> The dreams that we share,
> The love and the warmth,
> The stroke of your hair?
> For you've given us permission
> And called out our names
> To meet and to greet us;
> At last we can say,
> 'You've awoken to our singing,
> Recognise our signs,
> We salute you, dear golden child of the
>   Divine.'

I thanked my angel and he left just as fast as he had come. I sat there, wondering what had just happened. I read back what he had asked me to write – it was so beautiful, no wonder he wanted me to write it down!

The visits feel so much a part of me; it's like family popping in and out, like they are waiting in the wings (pardon the pun), but, at the same time, giving me space to live my life with my husband and children.

The great thing was, I was able to share this with

Paul – he is a great support and we are best friends. I love him so much, everything felt so comfortable. We often talk about why I have these communications. Why me? Where is it all going? At the time, I didn't know the answers, I just enjoyed the contact.

The years were rolling by so fast and the children were growing very quickly. In the blink of an eye, we moved to a new home and settled down. This is where I met my dear friend, Marie. We became very close – she is the sister I never had, she is like my solid foundation rock.

We threw ourselves into organising youth clubs and activities for the children in the area. It was fun; our friendship grew and our coffee mornings became longer. For nearly four years we were all happy.

Then, gangs of yobs moved into the area causing misery for everyone. The effects were like ripples in a pond, affecting our children – that was the last straw.

Marie and her family moved out, and my health began to suffer because of the strain. The feeling of things being out of control hit me hard. Even though the circumstances were different from years before, it felt like I was opening up old wounds again and feeling that same despair. Paul and I were at a loss; what were we going to do? Things had to change, but how?

One morning, after a sleepless night, I turned on the TV. There was a lady on it talking about her angels and how the angels had transformed her life. It gave me fresh hope, so I went out and bought her book.

By reading the book I began to understand what was happening to me and my own experience with the angels. I was so happy to find that other people had angel visits and magic moments just like me.

I began to put a lot of what I read into practice. I was now a woman on a mission, not a victim any more. Paul was delighted that I now seemed to have a positive outlook. I reminded him what my grandmother and Archangel Michael had told me years before: 'We will always help you.' I still saw my friend Marie – we were as close as ever and she shared my enthusiasm for my awakening to my angels.

I still wrote in my diary and I began to sit and talk with my angels. One night, I sat and wrote a letter to all the angels and my grandmother. I poured my heart out about my situation; it felt good to release it.

I knew it was no coincidence that I had turned on the TV that morning. That was the angels' way of giving me the tools to help myself. I began a noticeboard and gave each angel a task. We decided to look for a new home, and when I asked the angels where we should move to, I took care to ask for the specific location we wanted and needed to be in.

Hope filled me and the angels helped calm the storms around us. If at any time I felt doubtful, the angels would whisper, 'Have faith, Elaine.'

Having Archangel Michael's blue cloak of protection around my family and Archangel Raphael healing the situation, I felt confident. Miracles do happen and they happen to me.

My links to the angels were now becoming stronger. I got to meet many more, like Archangel Uriel, who showed me his rainbow light. He helped me with my writing and with the changes that were happening in my life.

We started house-hunting, but we were still at the

stage of wondering how we would do it. 'We will find a way,' I kept telling Paul, 'we will find a way.'

One day, we came to the last house on our list. The minute we walked in, my eyes popped out of my head. It was everything we were looking for. It was just what was on our list with the angels. It needed a lot of work, but that was OK too.

When we saw the garden – Paul is the one with green fingers – it was very overgrown, but I could see he was planning what to do. We hugged each other, we were so happy. I asked the spirits and angels to give us a sign that this was it. As we soaked up the atmosphere, two robins flew down to our feet. I had come to know my grandparents would come together as robins, so I knew this was the thumbs up from them. After sorting out the details, we moved in a few weeks later.

It was our labour of love and to see Paul create a piece of heaven was wonderful. Butterflies and robins would always be with us in the garden, everything that is blessed by the angels is wonderful.

I wrote a poem to thank my angels and the spirit world for all their love and support.

My Angels

My angels, I love and adore you,
I bless and thank you every day
For coming to me when I call you,
You're never far away.
Each day you bring a miracle,
Which brings a smile to me.
You just keep reminding me

That you hold me so tenderly.
You gave us a beautiful garden
To sit and be with you.
My husband's gifted hands were guided by you
To create a piece of your heaven,
To let us know what it's like
To be held, loved and protected
In your everlasting light.

Now, when we sit in our garden and watch our children play happily and safely, it makes my heart sing.

Smile

Each day I see my children, I smile;
The angels bring this miracle to me.
Each day I see my husband, I smile;
The angels bring this miracle to me.
Each day I see the robins greet me, I smile;
The angels bring this miracle to me.

I talk very openly about my angels and spirits with my children. They ask lots of questions and I try to answer them as best I can.

They come in and say, 'I found a white feather today, Mum,' because I always find my own. So I keep them in a special box and they put theirs in with mine. It inspired me to write a poem about them.

My Little White Feathers

Their wings of love surround me,
Each and every day.
They leave their little white feathers –
A surprise, a token to say,
'We are always with you, no matter what,
You are never alone.'
The joy of seeing my little white feathers
Is always a reminder to me
That I'll always have a friend in my angel –
That's very special to me.

Even though I never pushed my beliefs on my children, they respect my passion for my spiritual work. When they go somewhere, they bring back a book or an angel picture. Paul buys me new angels for the garden and if he has had a tough day in the garden he pipes up, 'I'm doing this for you and your angels, you know!'

Our youngest son, Quinten, is a very spiritual little boy. The faith and love he has for his angels overwhelms me all the time. His favourite is the angel St Anthony. When Quinten was born, we gave him Anthony as a middle name because of the love and respect I have for this angel.

If Quinten ever needed to find something, such as one of his toys, I would hear him ask St Anthony to help him find it. After a few minutes I would hear him shout, 'It's OK, Mum, we found it!'

One day, St Anthony taught him a lesson. Quinten was being very naughty; he was looking for his dummy and he was having an off day. My patience was, at this stage, beginning to pop. I told him that if he didn't behave, St Anthony would not help him find his dummy.

After about an hour, when we had cuddled up together, he said, 'Sorry, Mummy,' with the tears still wet on his cheeks and his big blue eyes looking up at me. I knew his little heart was genuine.

We held each other and I said, 'Let's ask St Anthony to help us find it.'

A few moments later I heard him go up to the toy box and look inside. He raced down the stairs too fast for me, pulling out his toys. 'Yes! Look, Mum!' he said, as he held it up in the air. 'Thanks, St Anthony, I love you!' he screeched. I cherish his pure faith. I would love him to hold on tight to it with both hands for ever, for I know St Anthony will never leave him.

A friend of mine came to see me one day; she felt she needed some guidance. Her life was in a mess and she didn't know which road to take, so she wanted me to ask the angels. As I tuned in, loving messages flowed in for her, but there was something special they wanted me to write for her. They suggested she keep it in a frame near her bed so she would always be reminded of their love and guidance for her.

Crossroads

When you reach a crossroad in your life
And each road looks the same
And you're full of doubts and anguish,
Your heart is in such pain.
You look around for a friend
And no one will come
To help decide which road to go,
For you to walk upon.
But your guardian angel is with you
In every single thought –
Just waiting for you to ask them
To help you with your walk.
You see your life won't be easy –
Paved with rose and gold –
But your angel will always guide you
And bring you safely home.

It was a wonderful reading – she felt so much better and she keeps her very special angel poem on her bedside table.

I feel honoured and privileged that the angels allow me to help others. When I see people in a lot of pain and anguish, the spirit world pops in and messages start flowing. When I see the person before me receive some peace of mind, I know my job is done.

I have lots of fun with the angels as well. I sit and ask them whether they enjoyed the movie the family watched the night before. I know they love parties because each time we get photos developed the angels' orbs are all over them. I invite them to everything we do, they always give me signs as well. They play with my radio, my lights, my TV – all different things.

A visual technique I use a lot to help me relax, focus and ground myself is to pick out one of my most precious moments with my family. I have suggested to others to try it. Every time you need some space, go to your precious moment. Mine goes as follows:

> We went on holiday with the children to Spain – one of my favourite places to be. The house is right on the beach, one step off the decking area and I feel the hot sand unfold around my feet. As I slowly walk to the water's edge to feel the gently lapping waves tickle my toes, I sweep the wet soft sand and I enjoy the feeling of renewal to my tired legs. As I come back to lie down, Paul joins me with a gentle kiss. We both settle back, quietly enjoying the peace and relaxation. The

children are still sleeping after the long flight, which makes this moment much more tranquil. How long it will last doesn't matter; what is important is that we are all together.

Seconds later, the children come rushing out through the sand. They are screeching with delight; the ocean is calling them. We sit to watch the glee and excitement they share with each other.

They embrace the waves with shouts of pure happiness. 'This is what makes memories of magic moments last for a lifetime,' Paul says. I can't agree more. We sit in each other's arms; it is just perfect.

We join in the fun for a while, then I go and get the camera and my diary. I sit under the parasol and settle into a cosy, relaxing chair. I capture them doing all sorts. They call out, 'Take another! And another, Mum!' I gladly oblige.

As I watch them create sandcastles and use their imaginations, a wave of love pours through me. How much I love each one of them. I look towards heaven and thank God for these unique human beings I call my own. My heart and soul are eternally grateful.

While sitting in my garden one afternoon, I was taking a bit of time out before the children came in from school.

The family of robins and some butterflies joined me. They always bring a smile to my face – it's usually a calling card from the angels and spirits that they are near. Sometimes we just sit there, other times we speak to each other.

I felt the breeze of an angel near my ear, which meant she wanted to tell me something. I settled back and she gave me a poem, this is how it goes:

It's a Miracle

> Come sit for a while and listen;
> Be still, look around
> At the magic we call a miracle.
> Who needs tickets for a magic show
> Which thrills us with surprise?
> For life itself is magic,
> If we take the time to see
> All the wondrous joys it brings –
> To see a flower bud open,
> To see a baby born,
> Be still, look and listen,
> That's a miracle.
> Make time each day.
> Be still, look and listen

To the birds, to the sound of magic –
No, it's a miracle.

*A*ll my poems are inspired by my angels. The words fly down on the paper so fast I have to ask the angels to slow down, while I'm trying to write it all. I don't know why they choose to give me a lot of messages through poetry, but I wouldn't have it any other way.

Sadriel and Eth are two angels who I work closely with. They are the angels who help to organise my time. When I ask them to help me get organised with my housework, because I need to get to the school on time and I'm running behind, I pause. Before I know it I'm whizzing around like a bee, I even have time for a coffee. Now that what's I call getting things done in angel time and it really works – try it out!

Quinten had a hospital appointment for an eye check-up. We sat together before we left and held hands. We were both going to ask Archangel Raphael to place his hands on Quinten's eyes. I saw Quinten in a ball of green light and told the angel whatever help he could give us today would be great. We opened our eyes and Quinten said, 'That felt warm, Mum.'

'I felt it too, son.'

After the eye test, the doctor said there was an improvement; I mentally thanked Raphael. Walking to the car park afterwards, Quinten said, 'Look, Mum, over there. Raphael came in his own van.' I looked closer; on the side of the van, big bold writing said, 'Raphael's Healing Centre'. 'Where is he, Mum? He isn't in it.' And, before I could answer him, he added, 'He is probably helping someone else.'

'Yes, son,' I said, as I hugged him, 'angels are for everyone.' It was my validation that they are always there.

A friend of mine died in a house fire and, even though I knew where he was and that he was still living on, I missed seeing him. One night, just as I was about to go to sleep I heard an angel asking me to write a poem and I knew it was a message about my friend.

Loving Wishes

No telephones in heaven,
No emails I can send,
No door for me to knock on
To help me find my friend.
One night, while I was sleeping,
An angel came and said,
'I bring you loving wishes
From your very dear friend.'

The following morning I was thinking of the visit from his angel and I was happy to hear he was OK. For I know, when he is ready, he will come and talk with me for a while.

I have been communicating with a very special lady named Doris from the spirit world. Her life was spent talking to spirits every day and her books are wonderful. We never met here on earth but I will settle for our talks from the spirit world. I admire her greatly and especially her natural way of helping people. I remember seeing her on TV, when I was a little girl, because I felt drawn to all things to do with the spirit world.

One day, I was reading her book and realised we are so alike in many ways. I found that unbelievable, it was great. She is also very funny; I laugh so much it hurts, she is such an inspiration to me. Before Doris contacted me, I had asked my grandmother to find Doris and ask her if she would be able to work with me. Now, if anyone could find her it would be my nan.

I was sitting comfortably, reading my book, while the boys were getting ready. Quinten had a race – he does motocross racing – so they were all busy and excited about the afternoon event. Paul came and opened the laptop at the other end of the table from me. I thought this was slightly strange, as he is usually too busy on race days to spend time on the computer, but I was so into my book I just carried on.

'There's an email here for you, Elaine,' he said.

I dragged my eyes away from the book, 'Who's it from?' I asked, not really interested because I was enjoying my reading so much.

'I'll read it to you,' he offered.

I nodded my head, but as I listened I nearly fell off the chair. My body was shaking; I was shocked.

'Are you OK?' Paul asked when he saw my reaction.

'Who sent it?'

'I'm not sure,' he said.

It went like this: 'Someone you admire a great deal is available to be your mentor. All you have to do is ask, don't be shy. Push yourself to make the first move and get the conversation going. Ask me to give you answers to questions and I will give you pointers or at least give you feedback on your ideas. You can no longer sit on the sidelines – the sooner you get started the better.

I knew Doris had found a way to get her message to me. I'm not really good with computers and she knew that I would not find it, but she knew Paul would as he uses the computer all the time. Now it made sense – he was busy one minute and the next he was reading me this.

By this time, the boys had come in to see what all the excitement was about.

Quinten said, 'I don't understand, Mum.'

'Sweetheart, a very special angel sent Mummy an email.'

'Did she really? I didn't know they had computers in heaven, that's just the coolest thing.' It was such an innocent moment.

I mentally thanked Doris, and of course my nan, who I had no doubt had a hand in this.

I have a habit, while sitting at my table – I wrap my legs around the chair legs and close my hands. There's nothing unusual about that and I did it as I sat, later that day. Only, I heard a voice say, 'Feet on the ground and open your hands.' But the voice was so sweet – it was Doris.

'I'm so pleased you came,' I replied. I turned the sound off my TV and left the picture on. She was telling me about the music and flowers she liked and she was so pleased I got her email. My TV started jumping channels – another welcome validation.

Another day, I was talking to Doris and I was asking her for guidance. She was delighted and she said I should also read the teachings of Silver Birch; I had never heard about this Native American before. So I explored this new avenue and ordered some of his books.

A few days later on 13 April 2007 it was the Grand National horse race at Aintree in England. It is a big family tradition of ours that we all get together and back a horse or two. There is great fun and excitement as we all scream at the TV, willing our horse to win.

I was looking down the list of forty horses running; I looked twice – the name Silver Birch was jumping out at me. I was thrilled; it was another validation from my friend Doris. It wasn't about the money, the message was more important. I shared the moment with everyone. They said he was an outsider of a horse and he didn't have a chance, but that was OK. Each picked their own and I stuck with mine. I put a little flutter on the race and then the race was on, the excitement was electric. In turn, everyone else's horses fell back and Silver Birch kept going. All eyes were on me – you could have heard a pin drop. He reached the finish line and Silver Birch won the Grand National.

'Why didn't you tell us he would win?' came the

roar of protests. 'Why didn't you put a big stake on him?' they asked. I tried to tell everyone that I didn't know he would win and that it wasn't about the money – I tried to tell them again and again. But I did win 104 euros and I knew it was a gift from the spirit world, which made me feel like I had won a million.

I was inspired to write this poem for Doris.

Doris

I have a dear friend in heaven
And Doris is her name.
We never met here on earth –
We talk from the other plane.
She gives me advice and guidance
When we have a chat –
When I'm trying to figure out a message
That I hear from someone who's passed.
So when the spirits come to speak,
Doris is there too,
Keeping orderly fashion,
'One at a time,' she'll say,
'Not two.
And remember, Elaine, to tell the living
We dearly love them still,
We're never really gone from them –
Just a whisper
Away, in the wind.'

A new telephone company was promoting its service. A lady's voice on the end of the phone was polite. I invited her to call to see me later that evening. While sitting, meditating, before she arrived, this stranger was suddenly in my view. I saw her hair – it was brown, to her shoulders and had a kink to it. She had a black suit on with a crisp white shirt. I had a strong feeling that she was being sent to me for a reason that had nothing to do with phones. When I answered her knock at my door, you could have knocked me over with a feather. There, before me, was the vision I had seen earlier. I extended my hand to welcome her to my home. 'You are just as I saw you in my vision,' I piped up. She looked at me with surprise and seemed not quite sure what to say.

On seeing my angel books and cards on the table, she asked, 'Are you into the angels too?' So we shared some stories. She picked some angel cards and I was able to give her a reading. I told her I could see the passenger seat of her car and it was in a bit of a mess – papers and books and empty coffee cups everywhere – and that she needed to clear it because Archangel Michael wanted to sit with her while she was in her car. He told me he would help her get organised and he knew that she was stressed out in her job.

'My God,' she said, 'I can't believe it! Come with me.' And she took my hand and led me hurriedly out to her car. 'Look at this,' she said, opening the door, 'just like you said – what a mess.' She decided she would clear it up. Even though she didn't get a sale that day, she agreed with me that she got much more.

A few days later she rang me to say that since she had cleaned up her car for Archangel Michael business had improved and she made more money than the whole team put together. I felt so happy for her that things had worked out. But I have a funny feeling I haven't seen the last of her.

My two sons wanted to play hurling together, but could not find a ball. After all three of us searched high and low, Dylan said, 'Ask the angels to help us, Mum.' I called them in with St Anthony and they told me to look behind the sofa. I was sure I had looked there already, but I trusted the feeling and, sure enough, there it was.

'Thanks, angels!' the boys shouted. They were as pleased as punch as they went out.

Five minutes later, Dylan came running in. 'Look, Mum, the angels found us two more balls in the field.' I truly believe the angels wanted to play too.

Another precious prayer given to me by the angels:

Precious Child

You're the seed in the earth that God has sowed,
We are sent to protect you as you unfold.
Every new chapter that appears is a new part of you;
We'll help nourish and feed the gift of life to you.
Each step we take with you
And if we see you quivering,
We're there to still you.
When you fully bloom in all your glory
To be admired and held – to love so dearly –
You will never stop growing because the wisdom within
Is from the Almighty and us angels, a pleasure given.
Continue on your life's path, grow and learn,
Remember to share. You are not far from home,
For when you call we hear your plea –
We bring light to a situation and comfort thee.

It was the twenty-first anniversary of my grandmother's death; I prayed for her and spoke to her, as I do every day. But I still miss her so very much. I had a reading done that day with a friend of mine, who is a medium, and she brought my grandmother through. She was holding a yellow daffodil – her favourite flower – and a wonderful reunion followed.

Later that day, I asked Nan to give me a sign, but I went about my day as usual. On returning from collecting my son from school, he was eager to change his clothes so he could go out to play. As I held his hand, going up to his room, there on the floor in front of us was a beautiful white feather. I was so full of love and pride as Quinten said, 'Look, Mum, the angels left us one of their feathers today.' I knew it was the sign that I had asked my nan for. As I watched my little boy put it safely into our feather box, I sat and thanked her.

The same afternoon, Quinten came in from playing and said, 'Look what I found in the field on its own.' It was a yellow daffodil. I hugged him so tight again; my grandmother had sent us her love.

I have often thought about the vast amount of wealth some people have, yet you see people starving, homeless, and kids with nowhere to go to be safe. And I wonder: do people with all this money see what I see? I'm not saying that some don't help, I guess they do, but do they do enough to make a difference in the lives of others? Ask yourself today: am I doing enough? If you're lucky enough to have so much, while others have so little, what can you do to help? Is there something you could do in your area, like build a play area so children can play like children should? Or maybe build community housing and give a family somewhere to call home? Maybe there is a plot of derelict land, right across the street from your office window, that could be turned into something beautiful. Maybe you could make a difference – you were given so much, maybe it's time to give back. Don't feel guilty for what you have, because you probably worked hard for it. Just give someone else a reason to smile today.

Another special poem the angels gave me; it's my favourite.

My Wish List

The angels in heaven were ticking my box –
Going through my wish list in twos and threes,
'What will we give her to help with her needs?
A fine handsome man
With a heart of gold –
So precious to behold.
We'll give them three angels
To rear as their own,
To love and to cherish.
And a place to call home –
To teach and to grow,
To love and to hold,
To cherish each moment
As inscribed in gold.
For these precious wishes
We give to you,
With love and guidance
And light too.'

𝓘 had just arrived home from the supermarket; Paul had put the kettle on. 'I need that coffee!' I said.

While we were chatting, the phone rang and Paul went to answer it. I heard him say, 'Well, I'll ask her.' Then he said to me, 'There's a lady wondering if you could speak to her – she sounds a bit upset, love.'

'OK. Hello?'

'Thank you,' the voice said; the lady was very upset. 'I'm sorry to bother you; a friend of yours said you might be able to help.'

I could hear in her voice that she was genuine. 'Well, I will if I can. Tell me what the matter is.'

'It's my son and his daughter – they had a terrible argument. She left the family home – it's been going on for weeks – she is pregnant and so young, everything is in a terrible mess.'

The angels were whispering in my ear. I told her the angels were telling me the girl's father was not happy that she got herself pregnant and it had caused a huge rift between them. I also mentioned a few other personal details. She was happy with that.

'My worry is that my son is going away on holiday tomorrow, so I want them to speak. If anything happened to either of them, the other would never forgive themselves.'

At this stage she broke down, poor thing. I wanted to reach down the phone and hold her, so I asked the angels to be with her. I told her that the angels said that when we had finished talking she should ring her son and tell him to make his peace with his daughter before he left for his holiday. I offered her a few more words of comfort and asked her to ring me and let me know how things were going.

About half an hour later my phone rang – it was the same lady, but she sounded so much brighter. 'Hi, Elaine. I rang my son and told him he needed to make his peace with his daughter. He said he received a text from her about an hour ago and he was going to meet up with her. This happened while we were talking,' she said to me. She sounded so happy. 'Thank you so much, Elaine.'

'Don't thank me,' I said, 'thank the angels.'

At this time I would like to thank my husband – he is my rock. His compassion and understanding for me and others is truly remarkable. When my friends come over for a reading and a chat, or someone in need comes to see me, he puts the kettle on and looks after everyone. I wrote this especially for him.

A Bouquet of Love for my Husband

It's not just today, it's every day that
I love you very much.
No need for cards and grandeur
To tell you how much.
You do so much for me,
In ways that only I know,
You hold my heart in high regard –
It's why I love you so.
I watch you work hard
And see you each day
Walk through the door with
Open arms and smile and say
How much you miss us,
With lots of hugs
And kisses.
Never wanting;
Always giving.
For it's a sure blessing

God gave to me,
When he was wondering
How much your love
Would mean to me.

𝒫assing a church one day with Quinten, he asked, 'Can we go inside and light some candles together?'

I watched him place each one carefully. 'Why did you want to light candles today?' I asked him.

'Just to say thank you to God and his angels for everything.'

My eyes filled up. 'You are such a very special boy,' I said as I hugged him.

I was doing a reading for a girl one day, who was grieving the loss of her mother. The lovely little old lady came to talk to us from the spirit world with a very special message.

Wonderful Blessing

There's not many miles between us –
Just a little step;
I stepped into heaven without any regret.
I had a wonderful blessing – having a
　　daughter like you
To love and cherish
My whole life through.
I know how special I was to you
And how hard it was to let me go.
I'm with you by day and I kiss you at night –
I'm the one who keeps turning off the lights.
It's just my way to let you know
Which little signs I'll send.
Be strong, my darling, and hold your head
　　up high,
For God and the angels love you,
And so do I.

Special Angels

I talk with my angels daily and I listen to
   what they say,
You see they're very special angels, who
   come to be with me each day.
I ask advice about lots of things,
I cry, laugh,
I enjoy their surprise which sometimes only
   I see.
They answer all my questions
And give me advice
On how to handle situations and people
   alike.
They tell me how much they love me
And what I mean to them
And how special our communication from
   God is as well.
They say I am an earth angel,
I have much to do –
To help all they send to me,
To bring angel light to every heart
That needs them too.
They allow me to hear, I sometimes see
Their wonderful white flashes
As they pass by me.
They allow me to touch
The softness of their wings,
I feel them when they hug –

It feels so warm and safe.
I know I'll never be alone
When I have an angel in my place.
If I ever wonder what to do
Or where to go, an angel comes to show me.
'Look,' she'll say,
'Just ask and you'll know.
We're always here to help you,
We're always at your side,
All wanting to help you and guide.
And remember, when a friend you meet
Needs an angel too,
Just take their hand and guide –
Let them see the angel in you.'

𝒜 little girl I know just started school and she was having a tough time settling in. I bumped into her and her mum one morning and she was crying; her poor mum was trying really hard to keep it together herself. The little girl admired an angel pin I was wearing on my shoulder. 'Do you see this angel? She is very special,' I told her. 'She sits there all day and looks after me and makes me feel happy.'

'How does she do that?' her little squeaky voice asked.

'I tell you what, I think she would like to look after you today,' I said and I pinned the angel to the shoulder of her jumper. She gave me a big hug and said, 'Thank you.' Her mum squeezed my hand and I stood and watched them go through the school gates.

Over my morning coffee, I thanked the angels for allowing me to help the little girl, but it didn't end there. An angel came and asked me to write something down for the little girl so she could say it every day before school.

Angel on your Shoulder

> There's a little angel on your shoulder,
> Who's with you every day,
> To comfort you and heal you
> And take your fears away.
> Each time a little tear appears,

> Remember who is there –
> Your little angel
> On your shoulder
> Will always be near.

I passed it on later that day and after a few weeks I saw them at the school. The little girl was still wearing the angel pin, but this time she was smiling. Her mum told me she says the poem every morning and she has settled down beautifully.

It brought back my own memories of when Quinten started school. I had spoken to the angels and asked them to make Quinten's transition from home to school and his parting from me easy, also to touch his little heart and to cover him in a wing of love and protection; I felt confident that he would be OK. But each day was an effort and heavy emotions filled us both. I cuddled him, wiped his tears away and it broke my heart to leave him there, for I knew his little heart was breaking too. I asked the angels why they let my little boy go through this heartache.

As the days passed, I lost confidence in the angels; I felt angry because they were letting Quinten suffer.

Waiting at the school gates for him one beautiful sunny day, my mind was troubled. On seeing him, though, my heart lifted. As I hugged him close, a beautiful butterfly landed on his shoulder and I knew it was an angel. I felt so happy that the angels had given us a sign that they hadn't forgotten him, they were with him the whole time. Also they reminded me that we are human and we must have our human emotions.

As I took the butterfly from Quinten's shoulder to

show him, I was able to place it in his hand. He was overjoyed as he opened his fingers to allow the butterfly to fly up to the sky. We both watched it go higher and higher. We were so excited because we knew that was the day we had held an angel.

This is Quinten's poem:

Hugs and Kisses

> Collect my tears and take them to heaven,
> Turn them into gold,
> Make them into hugs and kisses
> For my angels to hold.

Grief is different for everyone. Even though our loved ones live on, we, as humans, miss their physical presence – being able to see them each day, to touch them, hear them, hold them – the pain is unbearable. I have seen how it affects children – their world is turned upside down, sometimes they don't understand what is really happening. I know this from my experience of seeing it first-hand in my own family. When a relative of mine died, her children knew she had passed, but the confusion of all the adults crying, phones ringing, people popping in and out added to their upset even more. Everyone brought toys and gifts for the children; it was their way of helping them through the grief and taking their minds off their loss, or so they kept saying. But over and over I heard people say, 'The children are young, they will get over it, they don't really understand what's going on.' I wanted to shout out, 'Don't be so stupid! Of course they know. They may be small, but they do have feelings.' But I didn't dare because I was young myself, but old enough to know what a load of rubbish I was listening to.

I used to tell the children that their mum was now an angel looking after them. The youngest would run around shouting, 'Our mum is an angel in heaven.' It made them feel important that their mum had such a special job now and it made them smile. Others looked on with raised eyebrows and disapproving glares, but I didn't care too much what they thought at that stage.

When the funeral was over and people visited less and less, it was then the children would ask, 'Is Mum here now? Can she hear us? What colour are her wings? Will we ever see her again?' It was heartbreaking to see and hear so many questions that they wanted answers to. That is why I wrote this poem, bringing all their hopes together, especially the youngest little boy who was only two at the time.

A Letter to God in Heaven

I am just a little boy –
I'm seven years old.
My mummy went to heaven
When I was two years old.
I don't really remember what she was like
Or how it felt to hold her hand
And kiss her goodnight.
I miss her hugs and kisses,
I'm sure she gave me loads.
Everyone says I'm like her,
But I don't really know.
My daddy told me a story,
I wonder is it true?
God, you made my mum an angel
To guide and watch me too.
Sometimes I get lonely, angry and cry –
Why did it have to be my mummy who
   died?
There are lots of photos in my house,
I look at them every day,

But there's a special one I really like,
It's when were at play.
This photo is beside my bed;
I kiss it each night.
I cry when I see her;
I miss my mummy's cuddles at night.
So I'm wondering, God, if you
Could give me back my mum,
Just for one day,
So I could hold and kiss her
And show her all the things
I've being doing while she's away.
I'll put my photo inside,
Just for her to see,
In case she forgets what I look like
When she comes to stay with me.

*F*orgiveness is such a huge thing in our lives; we live with it all the time, from the small act to the biggest. We all try to deal with this incredibly big emotion. Sometimes we bury the hatchet, but some of us can never find that middle ground. Some people take years to release it; others find it too late because the person they forgive passes over.

The pain runs through us deeply when someone wounds us. And I hold my hands up, I have wounded people with my words and actions. As to whether it was justified at the time, it doesn't matter – it still made me feel horrible and gave me another emotion to deal with. I do ask for guidance to deal with it, but the angels always say, 'We can't live your life for you, we will help when we see you yourself trying to heal the situation.' I suppose they're right really, we have to find our own way or we would not learn how to forgive.

I remember one time, a few weeks before Christmas, I had fallen out with someone I was close to. We exchanged cruel words – equally, I have to say. Anyone who knows me will tell you that I love Christmas: the children writing Santa letters, the excitement of waiting for Christmas morning, shopping for gifts, ordering the festive hamper, the whole thing – especially putting the Christmas tree up in all its glory. It makes me dizzy with excitement. It's a family tradition that we all help to decorate the tree. Over the years, the children would make something in school for their trees at home and every year the memories would come flooding out of the boxes. It's so precious, I always start crying. I have to take regular moments out just to watch each of them and say thank you to God for giving me this precious time to share with them. When my children ask me, 'Is there some gift you really want for Christmas this year, Mum?' I always say, 'I have everything I need right here.' But they always put a surprise under the tree for me. They don't realise that just to have each one of them with me is worth so much more, but I do appreciate the effort they make.

When the tree was complete, Paul said, 'Turn the lights down.' One, two, three: the tree lights sparkled beautifully. The children were jumping with excitement. Wow! It did look a picture – another precious memory stored to relive another day.

Paul and I settled down after the children went off to bed and I thought about how lucky I am and about the person I was having issues with and for a moment I felt compassion towards them. They were alone and didn't have much joy in their life. 'I don't know what to do,' I said to Paul.

'Well,' he said, 'I can't help you with this, you have to be at peace and happy with the decision you make. There's no point in going over and over what you said or didn't say. What do you really want?'

What do I really want? Good question, I thought. I felt pain in my life and it was up to me to do something about it – control it, not feed it.

'I'm off to bed, then,' Paul said and kissed me goodnight.

'I will stay a little longer, love.'

Sitting by the open fire, I looked into the heart of the remaining flames. That's what it's all about: the heart of someone in all of us, that's what's important. As I watched the twinkling lights it inspired me to write this poem:

Forgiveness

> You can't give love in a box,
> Wrapped in a beautiful bow
> And put it under your Christmas tree,
> Proudly on show.
> For in your heart is what really matters,
> It's time to give it for free
> To that person
> Who really hurt you;
> Place forgiveness beneath
> Your tree.

The following morning I rang the person I had argued with and we arranged to meet for lunch. I learned that they wanted to make peace too and I was so pleased because we could all share the magic of Christmas together.

Where would I be without my dear friend Marie? We keep each other in check and bounce ideas off one another all the time. We value each other's opinions. Marie is very straight talking and tells it like it is – it is one of the things I admire most about her. We carry each other through rocky times and we can ask one another to tune in to the angels and get some light on our way.

From time to time, Marie does an angel-card reading for me. I love it when she does this; the extra words of wisdom are fabulous.

If either of us needs space away, then we ring one another and say, 'Put the kettle on, I'm on the way.' If it is sound, honest advice you need, she's the lady for the job.

If you don't have a friend to share your life with, take my hand and let me be your friend through the pages of my book. You might learn something and be able to tell someone, 'It was my friend who gave me a message today.'

Remember to ask your own angels to bring friends into your life. Don't worry how it will happen, trust that new friends are on their way.

Parenting is a topic that brings joy, tears and laughter, I guess, for every parent.

When you are given the gift of a child, you are not given an instruction manual. You learn something new each day; like a jigsaw, each piece *should* fit exactly, if only life were that simple! At times, the piece won't fit in, no matter how many ways you try. That's when you find another piece and carry on until you find its rightful place. So with being a parent I always try to find different solutions to the things that don't fit. I know in time the right pieces will fall into place. But in the meantime, it's OK to try other ways because by doing so we learn. Maybe we get it right, great; if not we learn from the lesson. Our lives are like jigsaws and being the parent can be challenging. There can be a whole load of pieces that don't fit when you need them to. Each one of us is learning and the stages of parenting are so different. Just when I thought I knew it all, then came the teenage jigsaw – now that's a lot harder!

Having good role models in a child's life is very important. If you grow up without that direction and guidance, you wander around like a headless chicken. And when you have children yourself, it's twice as hard to make and find your own time. But you can. Remember that you can promise yourself to be the kind of parent that you would be proud of and offer your children the stability and love they deserve.

It took me a while to realise I am not the master of my children's lives. I can't feel for them, I can't think for them, I can't love for them, I can't live their lives for them. But what I can do for them is to love them, support them, hold them, listen to them, teach them and guide them. They are our gifts from God and we are truly blessed. I call many angels every day to help watch our children on their paths in life. Archangel Michael, Raphael, Gabriel, Chamuel, Metatron, Uriel and Cassiel are just some of the angels whom I ask to help my children in any way they can.

I do get my moments of frustration, at times, doing housework, laundry, cooking and being a family taxi driver. I was feeling sorry for myself one day and I decided to write down this poem about the way I was feeling.

The Forgotten Housewife

We are all little girls and we grow into young
 women
And before we know it we are married –
O what bliss!
Then come the children;
O don't get me wrong – they are all
 welcome,
But the little girl who became a woman
Is now a wreck.
Have I done the cooking, washing, cleaning,
 etc.?
Where is the time for me?
Chores have all my time and I am too tired
 for me;
Why am I forgotten?
Thinking back to my carefree single life –
O just to have one day for me –
I am quickly brought back with the pot
 boiling over.
I feel stressed; another wash ready to fold.

Just one day for me, what would I do?
My hair, a walk, shopping just for me?
I could dream for ever.
I look around and I know how lucky I am,
But I still would like a day for me –
The forgotten housewife.
I manage three kids;
How do others cope with more?
Tell me please:
Will I ever get *me* back?
It's not easy being a mum, doctor, nurse, counsellor and Band-Aid;
People go to college for a degree in just one of these subjects!
What are housewives – born geniuses?
I say it's about time housewives got a better deal –
Government funds for courses in all that is expected of us.
We deserve a break, don't you think?
Do other people ever think of the housewife?
Have you ever thought, for just for one minute,
That the woman next door to you who has children
Needs a kind word, a chat, a cup of tea,
An extra pair of hands, a friend?
No one told us the right or wrong way to raise a family,
We learn as we go along.

Sometimes I want to be that little girl again who,
When the going gets tough,
Can hide in her mother's arms,
But I am those arms now.
I must smile and comfort,
But who is there for me?
I get frightened too.
Some days I want to reach out and scream
With frustration.
I want to do more for me,
But I never quite get round to it.
I saw this image staring back at me
From my bathroom mirror;
O shock!
I feel old; hey, I *look* old!
My figure, well, to say the least
It's a bit more widespread.
I feel dull, I've lost my courage
To face the educational world.
Why? I wonder, *Where did I get lost?*
When I was single, I was having coffee with my friends,
Sitting nearby was a lady with her children.
The children were screaming and demanding, 'I want, I want.'
We all know what that feels like.
My friends and I were looking and wondering how this lady
Could put up with such demands;
She looked so dull and tired,
She was at her wits' end.

And I remember saying, 'Oh, if that is what
   married life
And having kids do to you, I want no part in
   it!'
We were so smug in our smart outfits
And the price they cost could have taken
These kids out for treats for weeks!
Oh, the shame of it! Well, if that lady
Could see me now, she would
Have the last laugh, I can tell you.
When I look at people today, I look inside
And wonder, *Is this mother like me?*
I love my family but I need to be me.
Have you found you? How? Which way?
Now I suppose you are wondering when
I was going to mention the male species.
First, I love my husband very much
But my inner needs, bless him, have him
   confused a lot!
Do men have crises, I wonder?
I suppose after all they are human.
Yours faithfully, the forgotten housewife.

I love writing, going over all my scraps of paper. Some things are written on old envelopes and on the back of shopping lists, because when I get inspired by a message or a poem I grab the first thing that's near me. I keep all this together in my journal. Putting them together for my book is wonderful; memories are brought alive again.

Archangel Uriel is a dear friend to me. I've asked his opinion on beginning this journey and if something doesn't sound right he gives me another way to put it. It has been like this throughout; I know he is looking over my shoulder and watching me type. Sometimes I lose confidence and say, 'Uriel, is what I am writing good enough?' I would then feel a warm glow and feel his rainbow light fill me up with encouragement and love, and off I go again.

My children got tired of me asking for pen and paper, even while we are in the car! I would pull over and write something down. 'Mum, we are going to be late,' I would hear. So they ended up buying me a Dictaphone – it is great while I am on the move, but I still prefer writing by hand any day.

Archangel Uriel loves music and he asks me to play a certain CD while we are writing together. It helps me relax and the words just flow down onto the paper. Even when I just need to feel him close to me, I close my eyes and feel his rainbow colours engulf every part of me. It always feels like a refreshing shower.

Uriel whispered, 'This is something sweet I would like to share with you.'

Special Guide

Take the colours of my rainbow,
Place yourself inside,
Feel the love radiate
From me, your special guide.
There are many changes taking place
That is why I'm here.
You've made me a friend,
Not just an angel;
I know you hold me dear.
Recalling all your memories
Is a pleasure not a task,
Keep going, sweet child, and write it down
These memories to last.

My tears flowed on hearing this and I hugged and blessed my dear friend for his words of encouragement.

On my first attempt writing my book, Uriel taught me a valuable lesson. I love pictures and I like to have pictures that reflect a story. So I downloaded lots of beautiful pictures that were just perfect for my book. I carried on, ignoring my friend Uriel, who said, 'You can't do that.' But of course I ploughed on regardless.

My daughter joined me one day. 'How is the book going?' she asked.

'Great,' I said, 'it's nearly finished and it is almost ready to go.'

As she looked over it, her face said it all. 'Mum, you can't do that.'

'Do what?' I said, all innocently.

'You can't just use someone else's pictures and use them because you like them. It is called copyright. And she went on to explain how it would make me feel if someone used my poems for inclusion in their work.

'But the pictures are so nice,' I moaned.

'Well, don't say I didn't warn you.'

I called Paul. 'Do you agree with Hollie?' I asked.

'Yes, I'm afraid so,' he replied.

I was devastated. I sat looking over the pictures that were so perfect. 'I'll take my chances,' I said and I went to touch the print button, then *blank!* Everything disappeared right in front of me. I screamed out, 'My work is all gone!' Paul and Hollie tried everything to find it but nothing, absolutely nothing could be found. They were feeling pretty bad for me because they spent the next three hours searching for it.

I went and sat in my room and called Uriel. 'What happened, Uriel? Why did happen? All of my hard work – gone!'

'But it was not all your work – you took that which was not yours to take.'

'Do you mean the pictures?' I said.

'Yes, child, you ignored my whispers, then Hollie and Paul, so I had to pull the plug on you. You must start again; I will help you this time. Do it your own way, the way you always have done, and the pictures will come in their own time.'

'Oh, Uriel, I'm sorry, I should have known better.'

'You have learnt the lesson. Now, never take what's not yours.'

'Thank you, friend,' I said and I felt his hug, then I went back downstairs.

Paul and Hollie were still searching, but were having no luck. 'Love, I'll get someone in to have a look,' Paul said.

'Never mind,' I said and the two of them stood there surprised. 'I just spoke with Uriel,' I said and told them what he had told me.

The irony was, I shouldn't have needed this lesson after the incident that had happened a few days before. Quinten had taken caps from his friend's bike. I told him never to take anything that didn't belong to him and here I was being taught the same lesson myself!

It was a beautiful Saturday morning, I had a lot of housework ahead of me and was wondering, *Where do I start?*

I opened the door into my garden the smell of fresh flowers greeted me. Archangel Apollo gave us his beautiful sunshine to enjoy. The housework ahead didn't seem so bad after all.

After my coffee, I called the angels of order in: Sadriel, Eth and Jophiel – she always puts the finishing touch to my mirrors with her wings. We whizzed around; it is like time stands still. Now I know what the angels mean when they say, 'Angel time is not human time, but it is great to have it.'

Bringing the last load of washing to the machine I was surprised when I walked into the kitchen. There were two robins on the counter. We all looked at each other; I knew it was a sign from my grandparents. 'Hi, Nan and Granddad,' I said, 'thanks for coming to see me today.' I loaded my washing, put some breadcrumbs on a small plate and I sat and watched them nibble away.

Now Tia, my little shih-tzu, was watching them closely. But she was content to see them, just like me. When other birds enter the garden, let alone the house, she makes the most awful fuss. But never when the robins come. She sees what I see, she knows what I know.

Sometimes they give me a message, sometimes it's

just to let me know that they are there, always. I am happy just to see them.

I had a dream one night – it was very special. I saw Archangel Gabriel in a garden, sitting on a rock. He was telling me that I would see and know many things in this life. I would help the living and those who have passed over. The next thing I remember is waking up. Going over my dream it left me with a lovely feeling. Later that morning, my mum rang me. 'I bought you a gift, could you call to collect it?' she asked.

'Is it an angel?' I asked with excitement.

'Wait and see,' is all she would say. I couldn't get there fast enough.

It was a lovely box; I was like a big child, honestly. When I opened it there was a beautiful angel, sitting on a rock. 'Do you like it or what?' Mum looked puzzled.

'I love it,' I said and then told her that this was the angel in my dream. It was a validation for me and Mum was so pleased to have been a part of it.

When I brought the angel home, Quinten came to see. 'Look what I have,' I said.

As I took the angel from the box, Quinten said, 'Hi, Archangel Gabriel.' He was so sure which angel it was.

'How do you know it's Gabriel?' I asked him.

'Of course I know who it is.' I gave the angel a kiss and found a spot to put him – another precious moment.

I remember, one time, someone said to me, 'Why do the angels pick you to speak to? Why not me or someone else?' I felt the negative vibe from her.

She went on and on, but when I could get a word in edgeways, I said, 'Angels are for everyone – I have my way, you could have your way if you chose to. Everyone is different.' But she was having none of it; the whole conversation was so negative. I decided to leave and come home. I would never push my beliefs onto anyone. If I'm asked anything, I am happy to share what I know. She made me feel small in front of everyone who was there. I know I should not have let it get to me, but it did. I asked Archangel Michael to cut the negative cords from this person and to help her in any way he could, because she needed some healing.

I settled down to watch TV and I felt someone touch the back of my T-shirt. I looked round, thinking it was one of the children or Paul. But no, it was my granddad who came to visit me from the spirit world and he held my hand. I remember, as a child, he had a broken finger that he never got straightened. I had forgotten about it until now. He told me he would always hold my hand through my life. 'Chin up, you are just as important as anyone else. Rise above people who behave in a negative way, believe in yourself always. You know what you know and you see what you see. Always remember my words.' I kissed his hand. His visitation that night gave me such reassurance. It taught me I can only help people who really need me; it is not my job to do battle with anyone. People must find their own way and I'll be there if ever she needs me.

Just as I was sitting there going over what my granddad had told me, I felt Archangel Michael come and sit near me. 'I have something I want you to remember,' he said:

Cuddle

>Cuddle into the wings of your angel
>And let me hold you tight.
>Let me dry your tears with a breeze from heaven,
>Hear me whisper in your ear tonight.
>Let me hold your heart to heal it,
>Trust me as I say,
>My child, I'm with you always,
>In daytime and at night.
>I fold my wings around you –
>You are never out of sight.
>I'll raise you up when you are falling,
>I will hold you tenderly,
>So rest for a while and listen –
>All is not lost or gone, you'll see.
>You've just forgotten how to get up
>When life throws you down;
>For every knock you get,
>I will always be around.

Now I hope you understand why I called this book Precious Moments, because times like these should never be forgotten. Everyone talks to angels and the spirit world differently; this is my way.

Lightning Source UK Ltd.
Milton Keynes UK
05 November 2009

145811UK00001B/3/P